To all the little readers out there —Z.A.

For the lovers of words and the creative spellers —K.M.

All rights reserved. Published in the United States by Doubleday,
an imprint of Random House Children's Books,
a division of Penguin Random House LLC, New York.

DOUBLEDAY YR with colophon is a registered trademark of Penguin Random House LLC.

Visit us on the Web! rhcbooks.com

Educators and librarians, for a variety of teaching tools, visit us at
RHTeachersLibrarians.com

Library of Congress Cataloging-in-Publication Data
Names: Avant-garde, Zaila, author. | Morris, Keisha, illustrator.
Title: Words of wonder from Z to A / by Zaila Avant-garde ; illustrated by Keisha Morris.
Description: First edition. | New York : Doubleday Books for Young Readers, [2023] | Audience: Ages 4–8. |
Summary: "Twenty-six inspirational words and thoughts from the 2021 Scripps National Spelling Bee
champion" —Provided by publisher.
Identifiers: LCCN 2022028965 (print) | LCCN 2022028966 (ebook) |
ISBN 978-0-593-56893-4 (hardcover) | ISBN 978-0-593-56894-1 (library binding) |
ISBN 978-0-593-56895-8 (ebook)
Subjects: LCSH: Vocabulary—Juvenile literature. | Self-confidence—Quotations, maxims, etc.—
Juvenile literature. | Children's writings.
Classification: LCC PE1449 .A88 2023 (print) | LCC PE1449 (ebook) | DDC 428.1—dc23/eng/20220815

MANUFACTURED IN CHINA
10 9 8 7 6 5 4 3 2 1
First Edition

ZAILA AVANT-GARDE

WORDS OF WONDER

from Z to A

Illustrations by

KEISHA MORRIS

Doubleday Books for Young Readers

IF YOU'RE HOLDING THIS BOOK,

you must love words, like me.

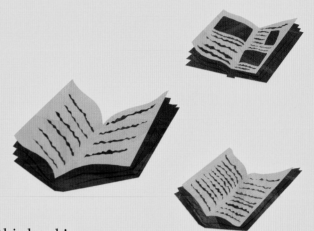

If you don't, you will by the time you have finished this book!

Words have the power to **INSPIRE**.

They cheer us up
when we're down.
They shine so bright
when everything feels dark.

Words have **RHYTHM**. Words **DANCE**.

They gift us thoughts and feelings.

What words are your favorites?

I've got mine—twenty-six of them—from **Z** to **A**, **ZAILA** to **AVANT-GARDE**.

I've made a **HOME**

in these words,

down

to

their

roots.

The door to the world of words is wide open.

All you have to do is turn this page.

I'LL MEET YOU ON THE OTHER SIDE. . . .

ZAILA means "mighty, powerful."

Z-A-I-L-A

"Murraya. M-U-R-R-A-Y-A."
—Zaila Avant-garde, spelling the winning word
in the 2021 Scripps National Spelling Bee

ZAILA means smashing all barriers in your way.

When people try to stop you from following your dream,

being **ZAILA** means not even considering it for one second.

ZAILA means not listening to people who say you can't play sports because

"you're just a girl."

ZAILA is just a kid like you,

and if she can be mighty and powerful, you can.

Anyone can be **ZAILA**.

You can be **ZAILA**.

Just put your mind to it.

Z-A-I-L-A

YOU are that amazing kid you see when you look in the mirror.

YOU are your best friend, always in your corner, even when nobody else is.

YOU are powerful. **YOU** are special.

A short and sweet word.

Y-O-U

"Today you are you! That is truer than true! There is no one alive who is you-er than you!" —Dr. Seuss

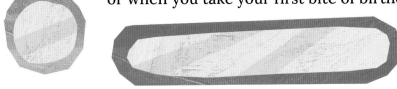

EXTRAORDINARY is that feeling you get when you ace your math test, or when you take your first bite of birthday cake.

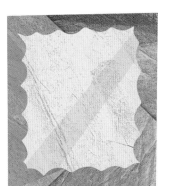

EXTRAORDINARY can be found in many ordinary things, like taking a deep breath of fresh air or riding your bike on a beautiful day.

EXTRAORDINARY is what you feel when you wake up and stretch out and think about all the exciting things you're going to do today.

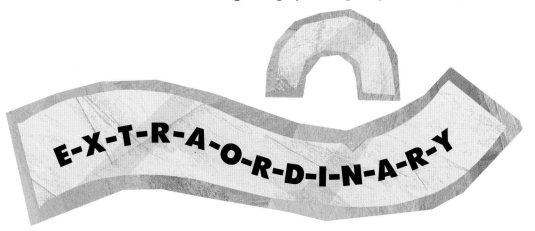

E-X-T-R-A-O-R-D-I-N-A-R-Y

"We must overcome the notion that we must be regular. It robs you of the chance to be extraordinary and leads you to the mediocre."
—Uta Hagen

Guess what! You are already **EXTRAORDINARY**.

WHY? The most important question you could ever ask.

WHY do birds fly? **WHY** can't *I* fly?

WHY can be a bit tricky.

Sometimes it takes a long time

to figure out **WHY**.

I *still* don't know **WHY**

I can't fly!

W-H-Y

A beautiful question

you should always ask.

"The important thing
is to not stop questioning."
—Albert Einstein

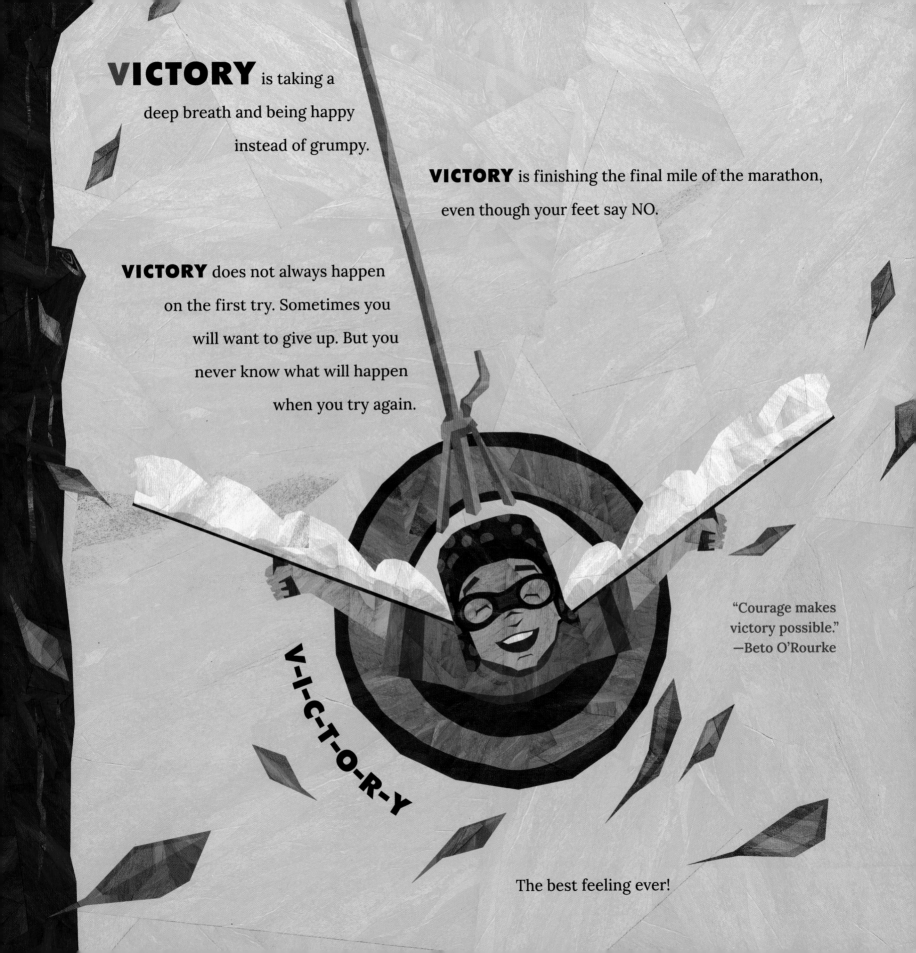

VICTORY is taking a deep breath and being happy instead of grumpy.

VICTORY is finishing the final mile of the marathon, even though your feet say NO.

VICTORY does not always happen on the first try. Sometimes you will want to give up. But you never know what will happen when you try again.

V-I-C-T-O-R-Y

"Courage makes victory possible."
—Beto O'Rourke

The best feeling ever!

UNIQUE is being unapologetically YOU, no matter what anybody else tells you.

UNIQUE is liking avocado with your cereal, even if nobody else does.

Being **UNIQUE** can be tough sometimes. People might tease you for being different, but you must be yourself.

U-
N-
I-
Q-
U-
E

"Never judge people by the color of their skin. God makes each of us unique in ways that go much deeper." —Ruby Bridges

Embrace every bit of what makes you **UNIQUE**.

TOGETHER is spending time with family, even that pesky little sister.

TOGETHER is the warm feeling that there is no substitute for.

TOGETHER is waking up in the morning and hearing Mommy downstairs cooking and your brothers and sisters happily chatting away.

T-O-G-E-T-H-E-R

"Let us put our minds together and see what life we can make for our children." —Sitting Bull

Without **TOGETHER**, very little can be done.

SACRIFICE is getting up early to go to school

even though you don't want to.

SACRIFICE is pressing Pause on your favorite video game

and going for a walk so you'll be healthy and strong.

SACRIFICE is helping your neighbor

water her garden.

S-A-C-R-I-F-I-C-E

"You can't achieve
anything in life without a
small amount of sacrifice."
—Shakira

SACRIFICE is always worth it.

RESILIENCE is not giving up after you lose the game.

RESILIENCE is getting up and dusting yourself off after you fall.

RESILIENCE is standing tall against all odds.

R-E-S-I-L-I-E-N-C-E

RESILIENCE. Take a deep breath.

It's okay. Try again.

"Do not judge me by my success;
judge me by how many times I fell
down and got back up again."
—Nelson Mandela

QUIET is what you need when the world is screaming.

QUIET can be whatever you want it to be.

It can be sitting alone in your room,

reading your favorite book,

or it can be meditating in the noisy cafeteria.

QUIET is relieving, relaxing.

Shhhhhhh.

Q-U-I-E-T

QUIET. A beautiful sound.

"The quieter you become,
the more you are able
to hear." —Rumi

PATIENCE is your friend

when a dream feels

far away.

PATIENCE says, "Count to ten"

when life seems more down than up.

P-A-T-I-E-N-C-E

PATIENCE can be hard

when your brain is hot and angry,

but patience is the cool, calm voice

that leads you to great places.

Hardest of all, have **PATIENCE** with yourself.

"To lose patience is to lose
the battle." —Mahatma Gandhi

OPTIMISM is making

the best of a bad situation.

OPTIMISM is seeing water

spilled on the floor and saying,

"Well, at least the floor is clean!"

OPTIMISM is looking forward to your

spelling test on Wednesday.

O-P-T-I-M-I-S-M

OPTIMISM might be a little hard sometimes,

but always try to see the sun

shining through the clouds.

"Optimism is the faith that leads to
achievement. Nothing can be done
without hope and confidence."
—Helen Keller

NATURE is everywhere.

It can be found in the heart of the city, or just in your backyard.

Go ahead—step outside. What do you see?

"In nature, nothing is perfect
and everything is perfect."
—Alice Walker

NATURE is in everything. It's in the lizard and in the bird.

It's in the gnarly tree out back and in

the cement crack you skip over.

N-A-T-U-R-E

NATURE. The gift that never stops giving.

MUSIC is the sweet sound of life.

MUSIC can make you feel happy, or it can make you feel sad, or it can make you wish your bedroom were a disco!

MUSIC is a beautiful way to express yourself.
Sometimes a song can say how you feel
better than you can.

MUSIC can be whatever you want it to be.

The sound of rain falling is like jazz.

M-U-S-I-C

The soundtrack
of life.

"One good thing about music:
when it hits you, you feel no pain."
—Bob Marley

LAUGHTER is riding a roller coaster as it dips.

LAUGHTER is chasing

(or being chased by)

your siblings through the house.

LAUGHTER is a gift you

give to yourself and others.

L-A-U-G-H-T-E-R

HA

HA HA

HA HA HA

LAUGHTER is

contagious. Ha! (See?)

Life is lighter with **LAUGHTER**.

"That's all you need in the world is love and laughter.
That's all anybody needs. To have love in one hand
and laughter in the other."
—August Wilson

KINDNESS is helping a friend up when she falls.

KINDNESS is sharing your snack.

Showing **KINDNESS** makes the world

a better place for everyone.

"Kindness is like snow.
It beautifies everything it
covers." —Kahlil Gibran

K-I-N-D-N-E-S-S

HA HA HA HA

HA HA

Remember, show **KINDNESS** to yourself.

JOY is going outside and seeing the first hummingbird of the season.

JOY is the sky during sunset when it is all bright pink and blue.

JOY can be something as simple as a sunny smile on your brother's face.

JOY brings people together.
Even the worst of enemies
might laugh at the same joke.

J-O-Y

"If you carry joy in your heart,
you can heal any moment."
—Carlos Santana

Always try to find the **JOY** in life. It's there.

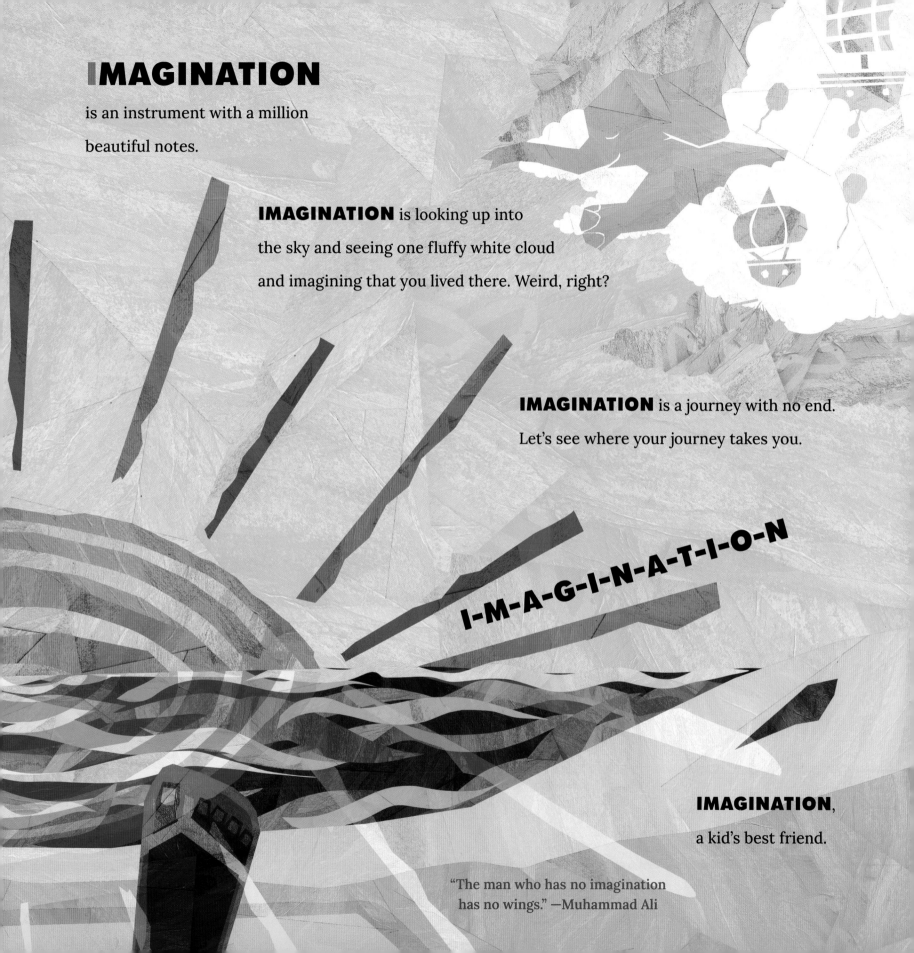

IMAGINATION

is an instrument with a million beautiful notes.

IMAGINATION is looking up into the sky and seeing one fluffy white cloud and imagining that you lived there. Weird, right?

IMAGINATION is a journey with no end. Let's see where your journey takes you.

I-M-A-G-I-N-A-T-I-O-N

IMAGINATION, a kid's best friend.

"The man who has no imagination has no wings." —Muhammad Ali

HOPE is something you must never lose.

HOPE is seeing not the dark storm cloud, but the blue sky after it.

With **HOPE** and hard work, there is nothing you can't achieve.

HOPE. One of the most important four-letter words you'll ever hear.

H-O-P-E

"If you go out and make some good things happen, you will fill the world with hope; you will fill yourself with hope."
—Barack Obama

GRATITUDE is the feeling you get when your grandma agrees to tell you *one more* story.

GRATITUDE is the smile on your best friend's face when you help her carry her books to school.

Always be grateful for what you have.

G-R-A-T-I-T-U-D-E

Just saying thank you
will make someone's day.

"Let gratitude be the pillow upon which you kneel to say your nightly prayer."
—Maya Angelou

FAMILY are your first friends.

FAMILY are the roots to your tree.
Without roots, there is no tree.

FAMILY will always be there for
you, like the net under a trapeze
artist high up in the sky.

F-A-M-I-L-Y

The most important
people you will
ever meet.

"'Ohana means *family*,
and family means nobody gets
left behind or forgotten."
—Lilo & Stitch

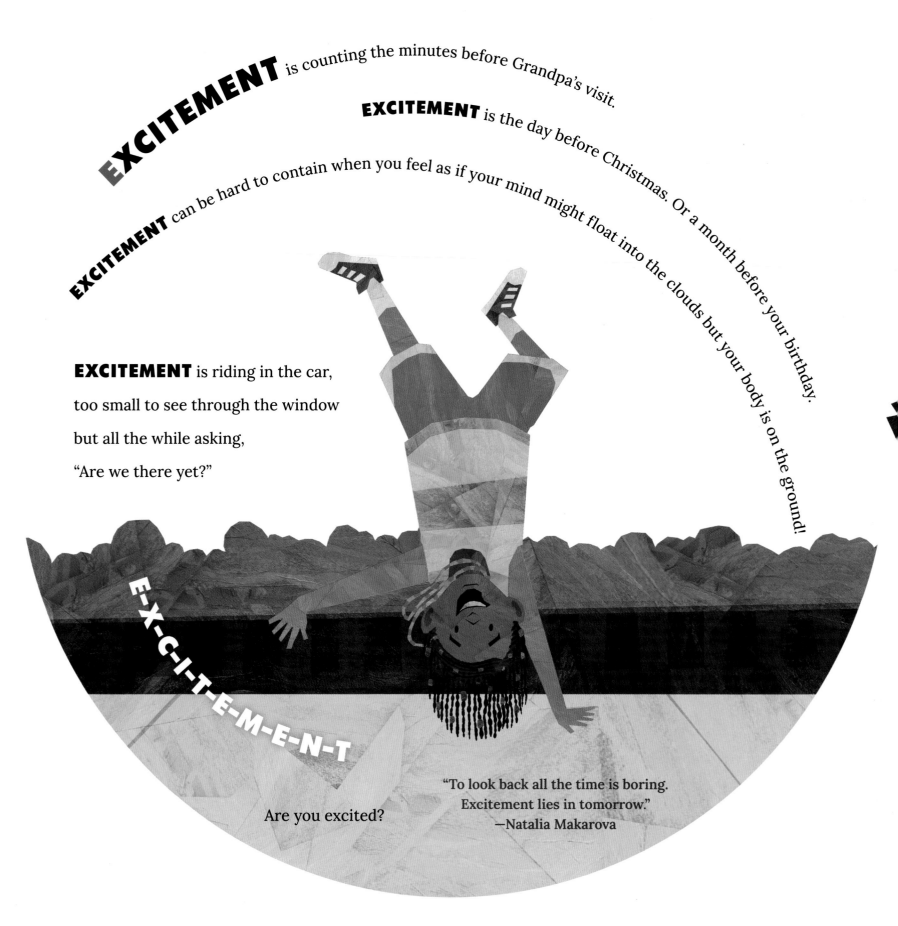

EXCITEMENT is counting the minutes before Grandpa's visit.

EXCITEMENT is the day before Christmas. Or a month before your birthday.

EXCITEMENT can be hard to contain when you feel as if your mind might float into the clouds but your body is on the ground!

EXCITEMENT is riding in the car, too small to see through the window but all the while asking, "Are we there yet?"

E-X-C-I-T-E-M-E-N-T

Are you excited?

"To look back all the time is boring. Excitement lies in tomorrow."
—Natalia Makarova

DREAM is
the word that makes
anything possible.

DREAM is a little kid in front of the giant bookshelf in the living room,
looking with wonder at all those big, colorful books. Not knowing how
to read most of the words yet, but still feeling something special.

"A dream doesn't become reality
through magic; it takes sweat,
determination, and hard work."
—Colin Powell

D-R-E-A-M

DREAM is reaching for things you can only imagine.

CURIOSITY is wondering if you can climb to the top of that tree.

CURIOSITY is imagining how the birds built their nest up there.

CURIOSITY is asking why the leaves change colors each fall—from crispy green to golden orange.

CURIOSITY is getting to the top of that tree and thinking . . . what's next?

C-U-R-I-O-S-I-T-Y

CURIOSITY is a branch to new ideas.

"Replace judgment with curiosity."
—Lynn Nottage

A **BOOK** is a key to an

enchanted world of your own choosing.

A **BOOK** is a best friend who's always there when you need them.

There are all kinds of **BOOKS**.

There are old **BOOKS**, and there are new **BOOKS**.

Long **BOOKS** and short **BOOKS**.

Fun **BOOKS** and sad **BOOKS**.

But one thing they all have in common:

They are magical.

"A book is a dream
that you hold
in your hands."
—Neil Gaiman

B-O-O-K

Read. Read. Read.

Who knows, maybe one day a **BOOK**

you're holding will be written by you.

To be **AVANT-GARDE** means to look up and see the moon, then build a rocket ship and go to Saturn.

To be **AVANT-GARDE** means to be at the forefront, always reaching for your wildest aspirations.

To be **AVANT-GARDE** means never simply walking the old path, but instead always finding a new one.

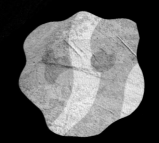

To be **AVANT-GARDE**, you must never listen to those buzzy little voices saying you will never accomplish your dream.

Channel your inner **AVANT-GARDE**.

A-V-A-N-T-G-A-R-D-E

"The avant-garde makes more sense to me."
—John Cale

What are **YOUR** words of wonder?

THE ORIGINS OF ZAILA'S WORDS OF WONDER

Zaila

In addition to being the first name of Zaila Avant-garde (origins: United States, 2006), *Zaila* is also a geographical term. It's the name of a historic port city in Somalia, a prominent center of trade from the ninth century through the nineteenth century. This city's name is sometimes spelled *Zeila*, *Zayla*, *Seylac*, or *Saylac*.

you

You comes from Old English *ēow*. There used to be four ways to say *you* in English: *you*, *ye*, *thee*, and *thou*. These forms of *you* were used differently depending on how many people you were talking to and whether you wanted to be polite or informal.

extraordinary

Extraordinary originated in Latin and then passed to English. It comes from Latin *extra-*, meaning "outside, beyond," and *ordin-*, *ordo*, meaning "order." It literally means "outside the usual order of things."

why

Why comes from Old English *hwȳ*, *hwī*. It's related to Old English *hwaet*, which is the first word of the Old English epic poem *Beowulf*.

victory

Victory passed from Latin to French to English. It comes from the Latin verb *vincere*, meaning "to conquer."

unique

Unique passed from Latin to French to English. It comes from Latin *unicus*, meaning "sole, single." When *unique* was first used in English, it meant "one of a kind." Over time, it evolved to also mean "special."

together

Together comes from Old English *togædere*, which comes from the verb *gaderian*, meaning "to gather."

sacrifice

Sacrifice passed from Latin to French to English. It comes from Latin *sacer*, meaning "holy," and *facere*, meaning "to make." *Sacrifice* has been used in English for over eight hundred years.

resilience

Resilience passed from Latin to English. It comes from the Latin verb *resilire*, meaning "to jump or spring back." When *resilience* first entered English, it was used literally, to describe objects returning to their original forms or shapes. Over time, it evolved to also mean a person's ability to recover from setbacks.

quiet

Quiet passed from Latin to French to English. It comes from the Latin root *quiēt-*, *quiēs*, meaning "sleep, rest, peaceful conditions." *Quiet* has been used in English for over seven hundred years.

patience

Patience passed from Latin to French to English. It comes from the Latin verb *pati*, meaning "to suffer, to endure." *Patience* has been used in English for over eight hundred years.

optimism

Optimism passed from Latin to French to English. It comes from Latin *optimus*, meaning "best." The terms *optimism* and *optimist* became popular after the French philosopher Voltaire published his famous book *Candide, ou l'optimisme* in 1759. It was translated into English the same year.

nature

Nature passed from Latin to French to English. It comes from the Latin verb *nasci*, meaning "to be born." The words *nature* and *nation* share the same Latin root.